6/14

DISCARD

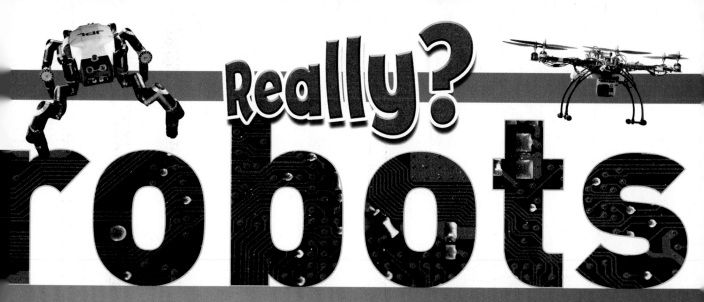

# Really?
# robots

## By Susan Hayes
## and Tory Gordon-Harris

**SCHOLASTIC**

New York   Toronto   London   Auckland
Sydney   Mexico City   New Delhi   Hong Kong

# Contents

Welcome, humans. Want to meet some cool robots and

ISBN 978-0-545-83345-5

10 9 8 7 6 5 4 3 2 1    15 16 17 18 19

Printed in the U.S.A.   40
First printing, September 2015

Scholastic is constantly working to lessen the environmental impact of our manufacturing processes. To view our industry-leading paper procurement policy, visit www.scholastic.com/paperpolicy.

# their inventors?

# Team Robot

**Vytas SunSpiral,** Senior Robotics Researcher, NASA Ames Research Center (SGT, Inc.). Invents and develops space robots.

**Dr. Cynthia Breazeal,** MIT Media Lab. One of the first social roboticists, and inventor of Kismet.

**Dr. Robert J. Full,** University of California, Berkeley. Specializes in nature-inspired robots.

**Dr. Hugh Herr,** MIT Media Lab. Creates bionic limbs.

**Dr. Vijay Kumar,** University of Pennsylvania. Expert in small flying robots and multi-robot formations.

**Satoshi Shigemi,** Honda Research & Development, Japan. Senior Chief Engineer of the ASIMO project.

**Dr. Blanca Lorena Villarreal,** Tecnológico de Monterrey, Mexico. Inventor of the robot nose.

**Dr. Andrew B. Williams,** Marquette University. Specializes in humanoid engineering and intelligent robotics.

# robot

I love robots because they are like us—they use their cameras to see like we use our eyes, and they use computers to think and make choices much like we use our brains. The great thing about robots is that they can also do many things that we humans cannot do. Some robots can fly, some robots are stronger than any human, and some robots are designed to go places that we cannot, such as other planets! In fact, robots can be designed for almost any job we can dream of. And they can even become our friends!

In this book, you will meet some of the scientists who are bringing these amazing machines to life and making our dreams of the future become real.

# world

Vytas SunSpiral

Senior Robotics Researcher,
NASA (see pages 42-43)

# Making robots

Imagine going to a lab each day to build a real-life WALL-E or C-3PO. Roboticists invent incredible bots that can help us in our daily lives, fly into outer space, and even think for themselves! Some robots are cute. Some of them are a little bit creepy and weird. All of them are awesome!

**What shape is a robot? Any shape!**

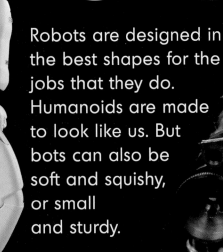

Humanoid

Soft bot

Flying SPHERE

Robots are designed in the best shapes for the jobs that they do. Humanoids are made to look like us. But bots can also be soft and squishy, or small and sturdy.

6

# Meet the scientists who are making bots today!

**build it!**

**You will live with a robot at some point in your life!**

Dr. Cynthia Breazeal works at the MIT Media Lab in Massachusetts. Her team invents robots that can teach, learn, and play like we do. She programs them to copy people's body language. A bot like Leonardo has tiny motors that allow it to make lots of different facial expressions.

## WHAT NEXT?

"If we can design robots that can talk to and do things with people in a natural way, it will be great. You won't have to make people read manuals in order to operate them."

Beneath Leonardo's fur are motors, cameras, and levers.

"When I first started in robotics, robots were big, clunky machines bolted to factory floors. Everything had to be brought to them. But then we gave them legs and wheels, which

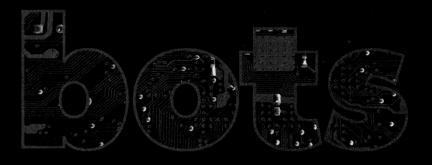

# bots

allowed them to move to their tasks. Now we're teaching them to fly, and the whole world is our laboratory."

**DR. VIJAY KUMAR**

(see pages 14–15 for more about Dr. Kumar)

# Robot basics

**Every robot needs a brain, sensors, and moving parts.**

Robots can look like humans, fly like helicopters, or crawl like alien bugs. But however different they are, every bot has the same basic parts. A computer "brain" is programmed with instructions. Sensors "see," "hear," and "feel" the bot's surroundings. Moving parts let it walk, fly, or lift things.

## Sensors
Cameras, microphones, and sonar sensors tell Baxter about its surroundings.

Wrist sensors show Baxter what it is picking up.

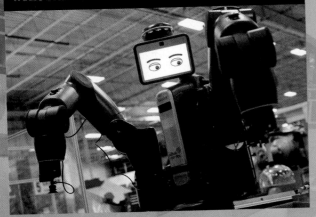

Meet Baxter, a factory bot. Baxter is programmed to load, unload, pick up, and pack in a factory.

## Degrees of freedom →
Seven parts of Baxter's arm can be moved. Robot scientists call this ability "seven degrees of freedom."

**The word *robot* comes from the Czech word *robota*,**

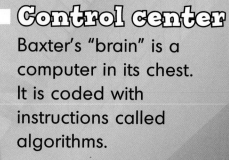

## Control center

Baxter's "brain" is a computer in its chest. It is coded with instructions called algorithms.

### There are almost 2 million robots in factories around the world today.

## End effector

Different tools or grippers for different jobs are connected to the ends of Baxter's arms.

### 90 percent of all the world's robots work in factories. Half of them are used to make cars.

# Work

"Earth person, hello. Welcome to the Robot Restaurant."

## MECHANICAL master chef

In Harbin, China, one restaurant uses robots as cooks and waiters. This one's in charge of making dumplings.

## FAST CARS

A lot of the work it takes to build a car is done by high-tech robots. In this factory, it takes just 80 seconds for robots to get a body shell finished.

## DIG IT!

**ROBOCLAM** digs quickly and deeply into mud and sand, just like a real razor clam does. Someday it may help lay cables deep under the sea.

razor clam shells

# bots

Am I out of a job?

**find difficult or dangerous.**

## BOMB buster

Stand clear when you take Dragon Runner off your back! It'll open doors, climb stairs, and dig around as it looks for bombs.

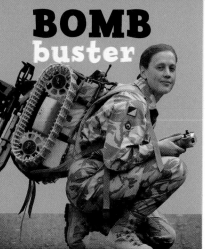

## SUPER STRENGTH

Strap on this body extender bot. This cool wearable robot will help you lift a 110-pound (50 kg) person in EACH hand.

## BOTS MAKING BOTS?

3-D printers can make parts for robots. The ZeGo bot has an arm that's a 3-D printer. Next up: a robot printed by a robot?

**microbot**

Lots of tiny microbots work together like an army of ants. They can build an electric circuit for your computer!

FlexPicker robots can stack more than 400 pancakes a minute.

## LS3

LS3 is a soldier's best friend. It can carry up to 400 pounds (180 kg) of military equipment.

# Flying teams

Imagine tiny flying robots that respond to one another, no human input needed. Dr. Vijay Kumar and his team at the University of Pennsylvania imagined just that—then built them! To make the bots, called quadrotors, they copied the way that ants work together.

## build it!

Dr. Kumar built the quadrotors so that they can sense one another and use simple rules to figure out where to go. Nobody is in charge . . . and no bot is in charge. The rules rule!

## formation, and they won't bump into one another!

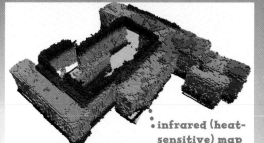
•infrared (heat-sensitive) map

### A-MAZE-ING!
Some quadrotors can make infrared maps. They use sensors to "see" where walls and doors are, so they can find their way out of mazes.

Each 8-inch (20 cm) bot has four rotors. They spin at different speeds, and the bot moves up, down, or sideways.

## WHAT NEXT?
If robots can sense one another, they can work together, too. Dr. Kumar says, "Today, teams of quadrotors build towers in the lab; tomorrow, they'll be building our homes!"

# Flight

## Is it a bird?    Is it a plane?

SmartBird

SmartBird flies by flapping its wings, just like a real bird does. On one test flight, seagulls dived at it, thinking it was real.

## SPHERES

There are little flying robots called SPHERES on the International Space Station. NASA is using them to develop flying robots that can assist astronauts with their tasks.

## Lost cities

This drone (a remote-controlled flying robot) helps archaeologists find buried ancient cities. Heat-sensitive cameras can "see" the remains of buildings beneath the ground.

## LIFE SAVERS

In many parts of the world, bad roads mean that doctors can't get to sick people. In Bhutan, robot drones are flying to the rescue, delivering medicines.

# bots

## Bee-size bot

RoboBee has superfast electronic "muscles." Its wings beat quickly, like a real bee's. Someday it may be able to pollinate crops like bees do, too. But no honey!

## FLYING CAMERAS

Want a good view of the action? Drones carrying cameras give us amazing TV shots of sports events.

## SHEEPHERDER

Battery-powered flying bots can be used to track and round up flocks of sheep.

That sheepdog can fly!

## Express delivery

Parcelcopters could deliver packages and pizzas to your door!

17

# Nanobots

Imagine a future in which our bodies are crawling with lots of tiny robots, keeping us healthy from the inside. Scientists are developing nano-size bots to work inside us and fight diseases. They could be developed to keep us from growing old, too!

One day you might get a nanobot from the doctor instead of a prescription!

### Just how tiny is a nanobot?

A nanobot is less than 100 nanometers wide. That's less than 0.000004 inches (0.0001 mm)! You could line up 1,000 nanobots side by side on one human hair.

## BRAINGATE

Sometimes people may [     ] paralyzed (unable to move) after illnesses. BrainGate allows them to move their robotic arms with their thoughts. Tiny electronic chips are implanted in their brains.

## Even now, tiny robots are helping people stay well.

## BLOOD CHECK

Some bots are small enough to travel through blood vessels. They can check the blood sugar levels of people with diabetes.

## ROBOTIC PILL

PillCam films your insides. Swallow it, and it'll take the same journey that your food does. It takes 18 pictures a second so that doctors can see if there is anything wrong en route.

## Nanobots now and in the future

In tests, nanobots are being injected into the body to recognize and destroy cancer cells. Next may be nanobots that can zap faulty DNA (the code that makes our bodies work) and keep disease from taking hold in the first place.

Wouldn't it be cool if you could make your legs taller or shorter? Or make your arms superstrong? Or have robot powers, like Iron Man? Robotics may have the answer! Someday, bionic legs could run faster than human legs. Dr. Hugh Herr is one scientist who builds better and better bionics.

**Iron Man**

Dr. Herr lost both his legs in a climbing accident. Now he builds bionic (electronically powered) legs for himself and other people. He can run, walk, and climb again.

## High-tech legs

**1** People who have lost their own legs use high-tech artificial legs. These are designed for different jobs, from everyday walking to sports such as running.

**2** Dr. Herr needed legs for climbing. He even built legs with spiked feet, which he uses for ice climbing! Not bionic, but still awesome!

**3** Dr. Herr's bionic legs are programmed to work just like natural human legs.

The **next step** is building limbs whose electronics become **part of the body** and are controlled by our thoughts and nerves.

Dr. Herr and his team in Cambridge, MA, study films of people running at different speeds. They watch in slow motion and figure out which forces the ankle uses to lift, leap, and land. This helps them build bionic legs for runners.

floor | flight | floor

## WHAT NEXT?

"We need to believe that humans are not disabled. A person can never be broken. It is technology that needs fixing. We're beginning an age in which machines attached to our bodies will make us stronger, faster, and more efficient."

Dr. Herr believes that bionics could end disabilities in the future.

BiOM

# Squishy bots

What if a robot could be squishy? It could crash into things without breaking, and bump into people without hurting them. Scientists are having fun designing soft, bendy bots that can blow up like bubble gum and find their own way around.

**MIT's tentacle robot**
This rubber bot has artificial "muscles" that puff up with air to make it bend and move through a maze.

22

## SPYBOT
This robotic fish swims by inflating and deflating its body like a balloon. In the future, it might be used to collect data about real fish.

Squishy, shape-changing robots can do all sorts of jobs.

## DELICATE TOUCH
Stretchy, air-filled robot fingers can pick soft tomatoes without squashing them.

## CLICK-E-BRICKS
These bots stick together like LEGO bricks. Build them up, take them apart, and swap pieces.

## Robot octopus
This bot is like an octopus tentacle. It has nonslip skin and a very strong and precise grip. It may be used for underwater rescue.

The tentacle is soft.    It stiffens, curls, and grips.

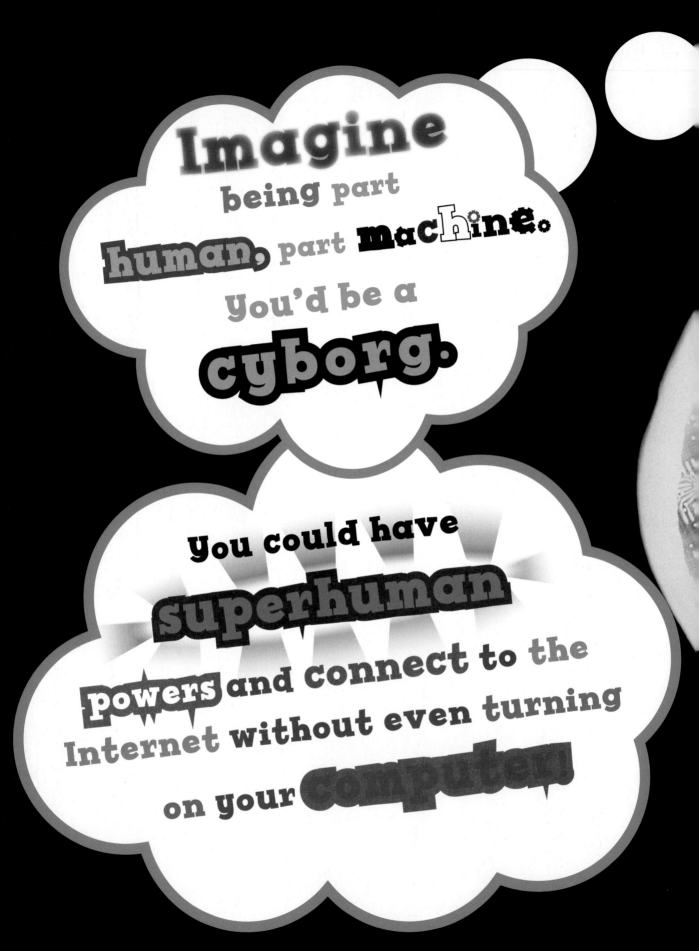

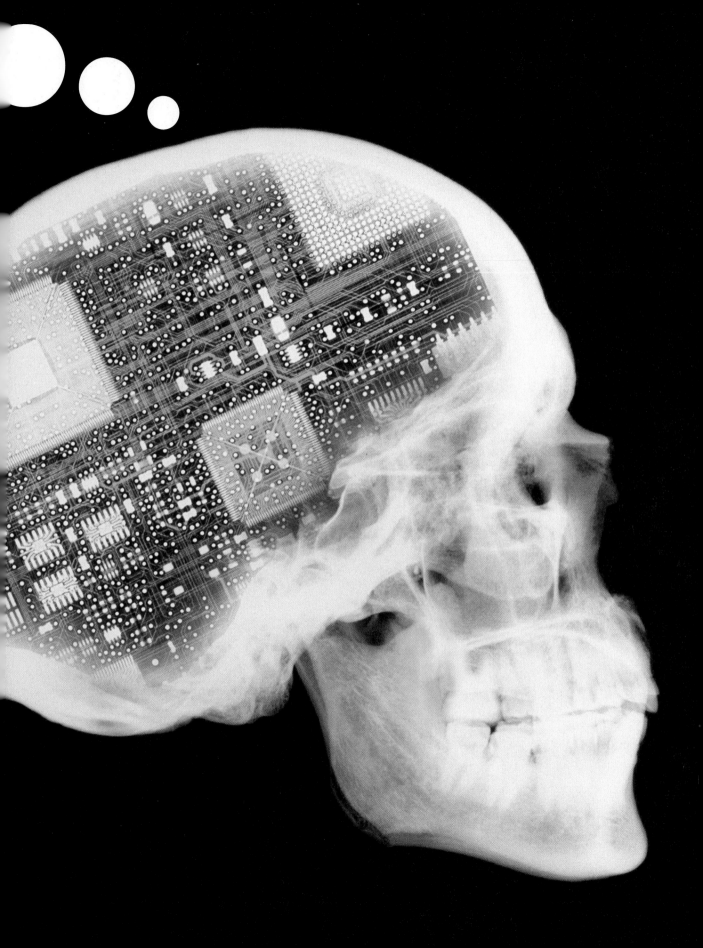

# explorer

"The challenge now in robotics is to design robots that can go anywhere on Earth and in space. Robots can't yet move through rubble from earthquakes to help first responders or maneuver through the sands of Mars to go down craters and search for life. Robots have only just begun to search deep under the sea, and we have not explored the oceans of Jupiter's moon Europa."

**DR. ROBERT J. FULL**

(see pages 30–31 for more about Dr. Full)

# Extreme

## Robots can go places that no person

Robots can't be poisoned or suffocated. They can be designed to withstand radiation. Robots can work in the most extreme environments on Earth and in space. Meet Atlas, a tough metal superman.

## Superstrong

Atlas could be in charge of saving your life one day! Built for rough outdoor terrain, it can drive a car, break down walls, and scale buildings. It is so strong, it can withstand a midsize wrecking ball swinging at its torso.

Atlas has 28 joints in its body. You have 22 in just your hand.

## How big?

| Atlas: | Average American man: |
|--------|------------------------|
| 6 feet, 2 inches (1.9 m) | 5 feet, 10 inches (1.8 m) |

Atlas is being designed to save lives, put

# explorers

would risk ☐ visiting! They're superhuman!

*BionicKangaroo jumps!*

## Copying nature

Explorer and rescue bots need to be able to cross difficult terrain. Scientists are inventing bots that can jump like kangaroos, slither like snakes, and walk like humans.

**A sidewinder robot climbs sand dunes by slithering like a rattlesnake.**

> **BOTS DON'T GET HUNGRY, AND THEY DON'T NEED TO SLEEP.**

**Atlas can walk slowly on uneven ground and run on ☐ flat ground.**

## Learning to walk

Atlas's creators say that it can already walk and run like a two-year-old toddler. They're working on helping it become a teenager!

# Nature's

## Want to build a bot that can do somersaults? Copy the

Many robot scientists are looking away from humans for inspiration. They're turning to some smaller but no less incredible critters. Dr. Robert J Full is inspired by cockroaches—yuck!

DASH is 4 inches (10 cm) long and weighs just under an ounce (28 g). It has six legs and can run over bumpy ground, including gravel.

**DASH** →

Cockroaches are great movers. They can run **upside down** and even flip themselves **upright**.

# secrets

## clever cockroach!

### build it!

## Tiny beasts inspiring tiny bots

**Ants: r-one robots** can keep together in a swarm and find a target.

**Bees: RoboBee** could pollinate crops, or fly around a fire picking up information for firefighters.

**Termites: TERMES robots** can build and repair structures much bigger than themselves.

Dr. Full's team watched a cockroach flip upside down, then programmed DASH.

**1** The cockroach grabs the ledge with its back legs and swings them around like a pendulum.

**2** Then the rest of the cockroach swings around, with the force of a human doing a bungee jump.

**3** The cockroach lands upside down under the ledge. It disappears from view in the blink of an eye.

### WHAT NEXT?

"We can take a lesson from nature to design robots that can run, climb, and jump. They'll be important to us in disaster areas that first responders can't enter."

WildCat CAN run, jump, and gallop over obstacles. MAYBE cars will LOOK LIKE THIS someday, and we won't need roads!

# Rescue bots

In 2011, a devastating earthquake and tsunami in Japan killed more than 15,000 people. A nuclear power station was hit. It was too dangerous for people to go in and fix it. No existing robot was suitable. So the DARPA Robotics Challenge, to design a robot that could work in a nuclear disaster zone, was launched.

**Competition bot**
Human-size CHIMP may win the DARPA challenge!

CHIMP uses three-fingered grippers to turn on a hose and operate power tools.

# DISASTER DANGERS

Leaks of poisonous gases and harmful chemicals

Explosions and burning gases giving off killer fumes

Falling rubble trapping people and blocking pathways

The competition is looking for the

**THOR**
At 5 feet, 7 inches (1.7 m), THOR is the same height as many adult humans. It can climb using its hands and feet like humans can, too.

Here are some of the competitors in the DARPA Robotics Challenge.

**CHIMP**
This bot can stand upright and move on all fours.

CHIMP has tracks on its "elbows" and "knees" for rolling over rubble.

**ROBOSIMIAN**
Cameras all over RoboSimian's body give it 360-degree vision.

# COMPETITORS NEED TO:

Drive a vehicle.

Get out of a vehicle.

Open a door. Go through.

Turn a valve 360°.

Drill through a wall.

Complete a surprise task.

Cross rubble.

Climb up stairs.

best rescue bot, to save lives in future disasters.

# Robot nose

**This robot can sniff you out like a search dog can!**

Search-and-rescue dogs work to find people trapped in disaster zones. But if there is poisonous gas, it is too dangerous for dogs. Dr. Blanca Lorena Villarreal was inspired to solve this problem. She decided that she would invent a robot nose to help in future disasters.

A dog picks up a person's smell and knows where to find it.

Two chambers, or "nostrils," take in air samples.

Dr. Villarreal lived in Monterrey, Mexico, when it was hit by Hurricane Alex in 2010. This and Japan's 2011 tsunami gave her the idea of building a rescue bot.

Spies might also use the robot nose, to sniff out enemies

sensor
...ects data
...t wind speed
...direction.

**DANGER!**
**Toxic Gas**

Dr. Villarreal designed her robot nose to work like a human nose. It collects air samples through two chambers. Information about the samples is sent to a computer. The computer figures out what the smell is, where it is coming from, and how to move toward it.

One day, Dr. Villarreal's robot nose will be able to find and follow smells to rescue disaster survivors.

## WHAT NEXT?

"Right now, my robot nose is still an experiment in the lab. It can recognize some chemicals. I'm working on making it recognize human blood, sweat, and urine. Then it could be used by a rescue bot to help save lives!"

Dr. Villarreal figured out how animals recognize different smells. She copied this process to create rules for her robot.

37

**Robots can explore Earth's final frontier for us!**

The farthest humans have traveled down into the deep ocean is 35,787 feet (10,908 m), in a submersible. ROVs (remotely operated vehicles) can get to the deepest parts of the ocean, but they need humans to operate them. Robots can dive deep, and they can do it alone! They can search shipwrecks for sunken treasure, find deep-sea oil and gas, and discover incredible new sea creatures.

Designers in Tallinn, Estonia, wanted to make a small, low-cost robot for exploring shipwrecks. They invented U-CAT, a robotic turtle.

U-CAT doesn't stir up lots of mud. The pictures it takes are nice and clear.

Crabster, a six-legged robot crab the size of a small car, will scuttle along

**ROBOT EYE**
SCINI's camera explores deep waters. It has discovered new ocean species, including a fish that swims upside down!

Robots can find their own way to depths of 10,000 feet (3,000 m).

**FIX IT**
A three-fingered robot hand "feels" its way through cold, dark waters. It's being developed to fix deep-sea oil and gas wells.

**TEAMWORK**
Groups of underwater robots work together to study sea life.

Just like a real turtle, U-CAT has four flippers to move itself up, down, forward, and backward.

In 2013, SCINI swam beneath Antarctica's ice. It found a new species of anemone.

**NASA'S Curiosity robot is on MARS right now.** It's digging around, looking for evidence of **LIFE.**

# Super Ball Bot

**NASA is designing a space robot to roll around Titan—**

In 1966, a robot visited the Moon. Since then, newer robots have visited planets, moons, comets, and asteroids. But a metal robot traveling at 19,000 miles per hour (30,600 kph) is tricky to land! Parachutes and air bags aren't enough to soften the bump. So Vytas SunSpiral and his team at NASA are developing Super Ball Bot—a collapsible robot that can crash-land and spring back into shape.

Super Ball Bot could explore Saturn's moon Titan without getting stuck in its lakes, mud, and uneven ground.

## Space robot timeline

These bots have all been busy

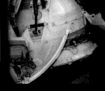
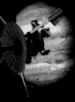
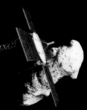

| 1966 | 1970 | 1971 | 1995 | 2001 | 2005 |
|------|------|------|------|------|------|
| LUNA 9 | VENERA 7 | MARS 2 | GALILEO | NEAR SHOEMAKER | HUYGENS |
| **Our Moon** | **Venus** | **Mars** | **Jupiter** | **Asteroid: Eros Shoemaker** | **Titan** |

This toy is like Super Ball Bot. It can be squished, but it'll always spring back into shape.

**Saturn's largest moon.**

# build it!

Super Ball Bot is designed to collapse when it lands on a moon or a planet. It won't need a parachute, because it will be its own cushion. It'll flatten to absorb the shock of landing, then spring back into shape, ready to explore.

**1** **2** **3**

**4** **5** **6**

sending us information.

**2012**
CURIOSITY
Mars

**2014**
ROSETTA
Comet: 67P

## WHAT NEXT?
"We're working on sending many ball bots to explore Titan, like a large search team. They won't get damaged or stuck like other space robots. They'll be able to roll off the edges of cliffs and down lava tubes."

43

# Transformers

Robot transformers are moving from science fiction to reality. Scientists are inventing robots that can change from one form into another. This robot, called J-deite Quarter, walks, then turns into a car and drives!

From **bot** to car and **back** again.

**Quarter size**

This transformer is only 4.3 feet (1.3 m) tall, but its inventors are building a BIGGER model. It walks at 0.62 mph (1 kph) and drives at 6.2 mph (10 kph).

Self-folding robots would be handy for space travelers.

**FROM CAR . . .**
The AeroMobil
car transforms
into an airplane.
Drive it to the
airport. Park.
Press a button, and
the wings will unfold.

**Flying cars aren't only in Harry Potter!**

**. . . TO PLANE**
AeroMobil can take off
at the airport or from any
strip of grass or pavement.
It needs only 650 feet
(200 m) of runway.
Bye-bye, traffic jams!

## ORIGAMI BOT

**00.00**
This bot is about
to fold itself up
and walk away.

**01.18**
Its legs and body
fold into place in
just over 1 minute.

**04.00**
In 4 minutes, it
stands. In 30 more
seconds, it'll walk!

They could build themselves into human shelters on faraway planets.

play
bots

"Ever since I was a little girl seeing *Star Wars* for the first time, I've been fascinated by the idea of personal robots . . . robots that delight us, enrich our lives, and help us save a galaxy or two. I knew robots like that didn't really exist, but I knew I wanted to build them."

**DR. CYNTHIA BREAZEAL**

(see pages 60–61 for more about Dr. Breazeal)

# Artificial

## Can robots think like humans?

Do you worry about smart killer robots taking over the world? Or maybe you dream of having cool robot friends like C-3PO and R2-D2? Intelligent bots can beat us at chess, drive our cars, and play guitar. When machines or computers copy intelligent human behavior, this is artificial intelligence, or AI.

**C-3PO**

## What makes up HUMAN intelligence?

1 The ability to learn anything

2 The use of reason

3 The use of language

4 The ability to have new ideas

In 1950, scientist **Alan Turing** said that a robot would pass the AI test when we can't tell it apart from a **human**.

**Nao**

## ROBOT intelligence

Today, some intelligent bots can learn. Some can reason and solve problems. Some can recognize and copy human actions.

# intelligence

## Computer brain

Some scientists think that we'll be able to upload our minds onto computers someday. We'd be superintelligent and no longer need our bodies!

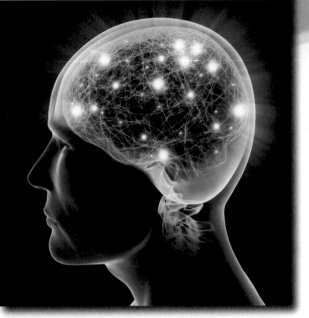

**Robots aren't as smart as you are—yet!**

The human brain is the most complicated thing we know of in the universe.

**R2-D2**

The human brain has 1 trillion cells. There are 100 trillion connections between them. The brain processes 10 quadrillion instructions a second.

**Diego-san**

## Like us? ➡

We might put human faces on robots, but they can't yet think for themselves like we can. Right now, robots can solve only problems that they are programmed to solve.

# Bot's got talent!

**Some robots compete with us at work and at play—**

## HIGH JUMP

Sand Flea can jump 30 feet (9 m) into the air. That's high enough to get onto the roof of a house in one leap!

## PERFECT COPY

Robots can copy famous paintings so well that art dealers worry about fakes.

## Looking like a human

This bot moves its lips when it talks. It also blinks, twitches its eyebrows, and moves its head from side to side.

## Trumpet bot

"Jingle Bells" is just one tune this bot can play. Artificial lungs pump air through its rubber lips into the trumpet.

**and they win!**

## CHESS CHAMP

**A robot's beaten the human World Chess Champion!**

### BOT breakfast

A German robot called Rosie cooks sausages and pancakes. It can also make popcorn.

## CHEER ON YOUR TEAM!

These robot cheerleaders won't bump into one another and won't fall over. Their arms put on a great light show, too.

## GOAL!
**Robots have their own soccer World Cup: RoboCup!**

**GRRR!**

Dinosaurs will never really be extinct as long as animatronics is around! With a little help from robotics, this dinosaur model can roar and gnash its teeth.

51

# ASIMO

## The robot kid that can help you.

Honda's ASIMO is designed to be the most advanced, helpful humanoid (humanlike) robot in the world. It's the size of an eight-year-old child. ASIMO can talk and use sign language. It can run, hop, dance, kick a ball, and serve your favorite drink.

ASIMO is powered by a rechargeable battery stored in its backpack.

ASIMO has two camera "eyes" in its head.

ASIMO "sees" where it's going using the visual sensors in its head.

Honda wanted ASIMO to recognize humans and shake hands with them. We can do that without thinking. ASIMO needed improved artificial intelligence. While shaking hands, ASIMO steps backward when its hand is pushed and steps forward when it is pulled.

ASIMO uses sensors on its head to "see" moving objects. It can figure out their distances, their directions, and if they are human.

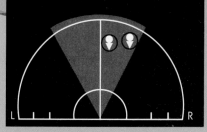

ASIMO adjusts its position to face someone. It uses force sensors in its wrists to adjust its movement and shake hands.

ASIMO uses its ground and visual sensors to "see" if anything is in its way. It will move out of the way of obstacles.

● ● ● Ultrasonic wave sensors can detect objects up to 9.8 feet (3 m) ahead.

Ground sensors can detect objects within 6.6 feet (2 m) of ASIMO's feet.

## WHAT NEXT?
**Senior Chief Engineer Satoshi Shigemi says, "Eventually, we want to create an assistant robot that can help people in their homes, such as the elderly, who might have difficulty moving about and doing things on their own."**

HONDA

53

# A human's

## Are you tired of all your human friends?

**5650 XZ-4A**

**E67C A8M**011014
3300166

35B62RN
GL44S4 20V

### A robot you
Geminoid can be made to look like you and move like you. It even uses recordings of your voice to sound like you.

### hitchBOT
This Canadian bot hitched 3,728 miles (6,000 km) one summer. It sat by the side of the road, waiting for drivers to stop and give it a lift. It tweeted about its journey.

### ROMO
This little guy is a smartphone robot. Romo moves around on its tanklike base. It can be a pet and a personal computer.

### Baxter

can do just about anything you command. Do your human friends do that? I didn't think so!

### PARO
A robot harp seal is used to comfort people. When it is stroked, it shows that it is pleased by opening and closing its eyes.

# best friend

**People can be such hard work sometimes...**

*U-nye-boh-doo? (How are you?)*

## NAO

This cutie is used to teach children in schools. NAO will react to touch and voice commands. It is also an extremely good dancer!

## My friend Furby

Furby toys talk, giggle, and play games. Their personalities grow as they're played with. The bots speak Furbish, but they learn English if they're talked to enough.

## Robot Pong

Robots can play Ping-Pong with you! You can change ball speeds depending on your skills.

## Tuck me in!

ROBEAR helps elderly people in Japan. It lifts them into bed and even tucks them in.

# RoboCup

## Can robots beat humans in the World Cup?

Every year, robot teams from all over the world play soccer in RoboCup. Dr. Andrew B. Williams and his students program their bots to WIN! In 2050, the winning robot team will play humans in the World Cup.

### NAO THE SOCCER PLAYER

→ 23 inches (58 cm) tall

- 2 microphones to "hear"
- 2 cameras to "see"
- 2 bumpers to kick the ball

Programming NAO is like writing down a recipe to bake a cake. A list of instructions tells NAO what to do based on what it "sees," "hears," or touches.

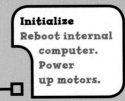

**Initialize**
Reboot internal computer. Power up motors.

**Ready**
Use vision to move to star position on soccer field.

## build it!

Dr. Williams and his students use math to program their robot's actions. The robot uses artificial intelligence (AI) to learn from its mistakes and get better based on past experience. This type of AI is called machine learning.

**WHAT NEXT?**
"RoboCup is fun, but it has a serious side, too. By figuring out how to make a robot kick a ball or score a goal, we're developing artificial intelligence. This will help us create robots that can help humans in the future."

On the **field**, there is no interaction with humans or computers. NAO can "**see**," "**hear**," and **kick** the ball.

**Penalty**
Pause. Let human handler move NAO to the penalty box.

**Set**
Pause motors. Stay still until referee gives start signal.

**Play**
Look for ball. "Talk" to teammates. Kick ball.

**MACH STRUMS** 78-finger **guitar.**

**ASHURA's 22 arms drum four times FASTER than a human's can.**

**COSMO's** laser eyes play **keyboard.**

Z

MACHINES

# Bots we care

**We're making robots that are easy to live with.**

Dr. Cynthia Breazeal doesn't like machines that treat humans like machines—beeping, buzzing, interrupting us, and giving us lots of information that we don't want. She makes robots that treat us like people.

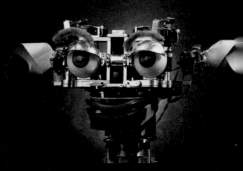

Kismet is happy when it gets lots of attention and new toys to play with.

## Kismet

is a robot that learns like a human baby does. Its different expressions tell humans what it needs.

**KISMET NOW LIVE: IN A MUSEUM.**

## build it!

...smet will get tired if it is given too uch information to cope with.

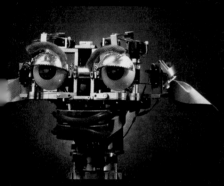

Kismet is given the same thing again nd again, it will get annoyed or angry.

Dr. Breazeal wanted to make a robot that could be part of a family. Jibo learns about the people around it, and recognizes their faces and voices. It can deliver messages, make video calls, take photos, and tell the children bedtime stories.

When your hands are full, Jibo can receive and read out important messages for you.

## WHAT NEXT?

"Robots have been in the deepest oceans, and they've been to Mars, but they're just now starting to come into your living room. Your living room is the final frontier for robots."

# Glossary

**algorithm**
A set of rules for solving a problem.

**animatronics**
Technology that uses electronics to make puppets or other figures move as if they are alive.

**archaeologist**
A scientist who studies ancient peoples and their ways of life.

**artificial intelligence (AI)**
The science of making computers do things that previously needed human intelligence, such as using reason and language.

**bionics**
The science that studies how humans and animals work and applies that research to the design of electronic devices.

**cyborg**
A being that has both human and electronic body parts.

**DARPA**
The Defense Advanced Research Projects Agency, part of the US Department of Defense.

**DNA**
The spiral-shaped molecule found in every cell in a living thing. DNA carries all the instructions that the body needs to grow and develop. *DNA* stands for *deoxyribonucleic acid.*

**drone**
An aircraft without a pilot that is controlled remotely.

**electronics**
Machines or systems that use many small electrical parts.

**humanoid**
Like a human being in appearance.

**infrared**
Related to a type of invisible light that has waves longer than those of visible light. Some types of infrared energy can be felt as heat.

**laboratory**
A room or building that has special equipment for people to use in scientific experiments.

**laser**
A narrow, intense beam of light that can be used in medicine, communications, astronomy, robotics, and more. *Laser* stands for *light amplification by stimulated emission of radiation.*

**MIT**
The Massachusetts Institute of Technology, a US university.

**nanobot**
An extremely tiny robot.

**NASA**
The National Aeronautics and Space Administration, the US agency that oversees space travel and research.

**program**
To give a computer or other machine instructions to make it work in a certain way or do a certain thing.

**roboticist**
A person who studies robots and robotics.

**robotics**
The science of designing, making, and using machines that are programmed to perform tasks.

**sensor**
A device that can detect and measure things around it, such as heat, light, and movement.

**sonar**
A method of finding objects by sending out sound waves and measuring how long it takes the echoes to travel back. *Sonar* stands for *sound navigation ranging*.

**submersible**
A vehicle that can travel deep underwater.

**ultrasonic**
Producing sound waves that vibrate faster than what the human ear can hear.

# Index

# Image credits